A Guide to self love

AUDREY MARTIN-LEE

BALBOA.PRESS

A DIVISION OF HAY HOUSE

Balboa Press books may be ordered through booksellers or by contacting:

Balboa Press
A Division of Hay House
1663 Liberty Drive
Bloomington, IN 47403
www.balboapress.com
844-682-1282

Because of the dynamic nature of the Internet, any web addresses or
links contained in this book may have changed since publication and
may no longer be valid. The views expressed in this work are solely those
of the author and do not necessarily reflect the views of the publisher,
and the publisher hereby disclaims any responsibility for them.

The author of this book does not dispense medical advice or prescribe the use
of any technique as a form of treatment for physical, emotional, or medical
problems without the advice of a physician, either directly or indirectly. The
intent of the author is only to offer information of a general nature to help
you in your quest for emotional and spiritual well-being. In the event you use
any of the information in this book for yourself, which is your constitutional
right, the author and the publisher assume no responsibility for your actions.

Any people depicted in stock imagery provided by Getty Images are
models, and such images are being used for illustrative purposes only.
Certain stock imagery © Getty Images.

Scripture quotations marked KJV are from the Holy Bible, King James
Version (Authorized Version). First published in 1611. Quoted from the KJV
Classic Reference Bible, Copyright © 1983 by The Zondervan Corporation.

Print information available on the last page.

ISBN: 978-1-9822-6334-8 (sc)
ISBN: 978-1-9822-6335-5 (e)

Balboa Press rev. date: 02/16/2021

SELF-LOVE IS SOMETHING not given to us automatically. Building self-love is a process it is something that will not happen immediately but it will be well worth the process! I didn't always walk in self-love because for many years I was in a dark space. I hated life and everything about it. I never saw a way out and honestly; I began to live comfortably being in misery. I had no self-esteem self-worth or self-love. I allowed myself to feel disgruntled regarding everything I was withstanding on a circadian premise!

Can you imagine waking up every morning questioning God as to why he continuously choosing to allow breath in my body yet again? Who would ask God such a thing? A person with such bitter, anger and misery inside! I was that PERSON! My mother passed away years prior of the depressed stage I was in. I longed for her to come back and take the pain away by rocking me in her arms as if I was still her baby. I needed her to tell me everything was going to be ok. I needed to feel my mother's love. I felt I'd lost my power to survive. I felt as if I had already perished! Nevertheless, I awoke one morning crying out to God in a way like never before and it wasn't until that day nearly three years ago that my life began to change in a way unimaginable. I began to see my life as God saw it. "For God so loved the world that he gave his only begotten son, that whoever believes in him should not perish but have everlasting life..." (John 3:16, KJV). It is my opinion; God does not want us to live a life of worthlessness. God is love therefore we are love and as we continue to follow and trust him, we can begin to see ourselves the way God intended. God wants us to have an everlasting life filled with happiness and joy it is not his will for us to live a life of despair. Building self-love is a choice. During years of depression, I never allowed myself to see any light in my dark world let alone self-love. Although I was in darkness, I carried it very well so much so that I was still attending church and went to work as if everything was well in my life. I was dying inside and no one ever knew but God as he knows all things about us because he created each and every one of us. Believe it or not, I didn't want God's help I wanted to remain in my comfort zone of hating life. I wanted to drown in my own misery. Wow, doesn't that sound strange for a person such as myself who didn't want Gods help in allowing me to see that life is more than worth living!

Moreover, it was not up-till that day, nearly 3 years ago, that I set about surrendering unto God! In turn, he began to move in my life in such a way that I actually began enjoying my life with such unconditional love for myself! I would like to share with my audience specific tools used on my journey to self-love! Self-love is the empowerment needed to forgo in hopes of improving relationships as well as self-improvement. It is my hope in writing this book, that I may help him or her on their self-love journey ! I feel the time is NOW for change especially due to the unexpected pandemic that arose and changed our lives in a way that we are now isolated from people! This situation has given us more than enough time for some self-examination! Please note applying some, if not all the instruments given will be beneficial on your journey to self-love. I myself, utilize the same tools day-to-day because I am determined to master this much needed journey! I have written down tools as a guide to help you on your self-love journey.

1

SPEND TIME WITH God! It is essential that him or her start their morning spending time with God. In doing this, you set the atmosphere as to how you choose to begin your day. "And when he had sent the multitudes away, He went up on the mountain by himself to pray. Now when evening came, He was alone there..." (Matthew 14:23, KJV). It is my opinion, that even Jesus himself knew the importance of spending time with God. While being in God's Presence there's joy, strength, peace and love." And the peace of God, which surpasses all understanding, will guard your hearts and minds through Jesus Christ..." (Philippian 4:7, KJV). This will be something that you can carry in your heart and spirit throughout the day and observe the way in which your day will be productive.

2

PRACTICE ON FORGIVING people that have hurt and wronged you in any kind of way." And be ye kind one to another, tenderhearted, forgiving one another, even as God in Christ forgave you..." (Ephesians 4:32, KJV). Not only should we practice on forgiving, it will be impossible for God to forgive us which will make it difficult to live a life of freeness. A life of self-love and self-worth. A life that you will be happy to be living. Did you know that carrying unforgiveness in your heart, can make you physically sick? According to John Hopkins Medicine, studies have found that the act of forgiveness can reap huge rewards for your health, lowering the risk of heart attack; improving cholesterol levels and sleep; and reducing pain, blood pressure, and levels of anxiety, depression and stress. I personally can attest to this as being a fact. I was in the ER often for anxiety, panic attacks, high blood pressure and endured unbearable headaches! It is my belief, holding unforgiveness in your heart affects your physical being! While I understand forgiving a person may not come easy. Still and all, in order to advance in your journey to self love, it's a necessity to began walking in unforgiveness!

3

SET GOALS FOR yourself and achieve them. Keep in mind that it is important to set goals within your growth. Set goals you know will be able to be accomplished within the time frame set. In other words, do not try to set a goal of losing 20 pounds in 2 days or set a goal to be married within 3 weeks.

These goals are almost unattainable to extend. However, setting goals within your growth allow you to manage them with such optimism of feeling prodigious within!! The reasoning of knowing that you are capable of achieving certain goals set, the further you are in your walk to self-love!

4

WRITE ENCOURAGING NOTES to oneself and hang them in an area in which you frequent every day. It's imperative that we realize that we are capable of encouraging and uplifting self. You are who you say you are!!!!! For the past 2.5 years, I write encouraging notes and tape them on my mirror.

Notes such as; "You are beautiful" You are smart God loves you. I choose to read these notes daily to get it in my mind and spirit as a reminder of how worthy within I feel and it's a good feeling because for years, I felt NOTHING!!!!!!!

5

STOP BEING IN competition with people and the world. I believe all social media platforms play a vital role in how we view ourselves!! There's many glamour and riches shown on a daily basis. Some of us tend to want what everyone else has just because they think him or her is happy with life due to having money and material things. Some of us will do anything necessary just to fit in where they really don't belong.

I wonder how many of us thought about the price in which the riches came. I know of some people that have everything imaginable but dislike their life strongly. I remember a time where I wanted badly to be this one particular person. Everything she had I wanted. Stop looking for acceptance in other people when you can't even accept the person you are. I was looking to be accepted! In doing this, I accumulated many credit cards in which they were all in default months later after charging half of everything I owned not realizing charging meant yet another bill. "Wow" to think I actually went into debt trying to live like someone else who in all reality never acknowledged me as a friend. I was so desperate to be noticed! Months later, this person I had much admiration for became extremely depressed and that's when I understood the outward appearance can be misleading! The only person to be competitive with is SELF! The most major fragment in competing with yourself is the capability in setting your own worth and values!

6

UNDERSTAND THAT ITS ok to say NO. We must realize and know that saying NO does not mean you're being selfish or mean, it simply means you are choosing to take yet another change in life. This took me many years to eliminate because I felt that saying NO would automatically make people not want to be bothered with me and at the time, I lived to be accepted from people. When you're living in a dark world as I was, you did anything to feel accepted with the lack of accepting self. What a wonderful thing to be free of using the word NO.

However, we must understand to stand firm and mean what we say. When my children were small, every other word was NO...

Howbeit, the bond that we grew as they began their teen-age years, it became difficult in telling them NO for my own selfish needs in feeing accepted in being a good mother! Still, once I understood the reasoning and I started my self-love journey, the word NO is used daily and it does not make me feel bad inside because I chose to change my life mind, body and soul and I'm living for me in a way that's not mean or selfish!

Understand that its ok to say NO and MEAN it!

7

DO THINGS THAT makes you happy. Spend a day with self. Self-pampering, Self-love. Find your quiet. We all live busy life's whether it's being a parent or working. If we are not careful, we will allow life to get away from us! I'm a mother, wife and entrepreneur, I didn't always "find my quiet". Between cooking, cleaning, working on my goals and business and doing laundry twice a week, it was a challenge in doing things that satisfied Audrey. It got to the point where I felt as though I was losing my inner being to appease everyone else's needs and desires and not my own!!

It would've been nice to receive some type of recognition! At times, I felt my husband did not value my desire to indulge in my QUIET!!! The compulsion to be left alone if only for an hour "Yeah Right". The moment I choose to sit or lay around in hopes of being alone and unbothered; my husband will in turn, ask me to get him certain things he is very well capable of getting himself!!! Anything to take me away from my comfort of having some alone time!!!! However, I had to find my happy place and it didn't matter who didn't understand! It was a must that I began doing things for myself.

However, I have learned that finding your quiet on a daily basis is much needed for the mind and body. Every day, I find my quiet because that's what I choose to do!

8

TAKE BACK YOUR power. For so long I felt that I had no power what a horrible feeling. I felt vulnerable it was almost as though I was walking around like a ZOMBIE! Heartless! One way I learned how to get my power back was to stop blaming myself for all the wrong things that was going on in my life. I had to realize that a lot of it was out of my control. I had to learn how to believe in myself all over again. I had to learn how to enjoy life!

I had to learn how to take my POWER back so that I can live my life the way God wanted me to. I challenge you all that's reading this book, to take back your POWER!

9
_____

BE PATIENT WITH yourself, now is not the time to continuously beat on yourself for all the things that's going wrong in your life. Choose to be patient with self-knowing that everything is a process and life will get better.

A lot of us have difficulty in being patient because we tend to want things done immediately. We must learn to simply just WAIT! According to Psychological Science waiting for things makes us happier in the long run. I have always been impatient because I do not like the thought of waiting for something good to happen in my life.

However, gradually I am learning the importance of being patient with self! I do not allow myself to do things of no importance and have learned to be mindful of the triggers that makes me become impatient. As I began this journey, I anticipated an instantaneous improvement within my self, marriage and my walk with God! Why did I think my life would change overnight? SILLY THINKING!!!! Nonetheless, I in turn had to grasp the concept in knowing that everything is a PROCESS!!!

Those of us married can possibly relate that even in marriage there's a process with lots of patience to endure everything that come with being married. I have been with my husband for nearly 17 years and within the years, we both had to learn to be patient with one another. However, the reality is I am still a work in progress because my husband tends to hit those impatient bones within. In the beginning it caused many arguments and separations but we made a choice to endure til the end. You find ways to fix the problems with a different perspective in trying to understand one another with a decision of making it work!

My walk with God is particularly important to me so much so that I became impatient due to my own clarity that life for me was about to be perfect. I felt a change should have automatically happened where I would be happy and released from the struggles of walking in darkness. Nevertheless, I had to understand even in that I had to be patient for I knew that all good things come from the Lord. "Every good gift and every perfect gift is from up above, and comes down from the father of lights, with whom there is no variation or shadow of turning…" (James 1:17, KJV).

10

REFUSE TO GO backwards reinforcing old habits. Once you make a conscious decision about changing your life, you must also make the same decision in refusing to partake in things that would allow you to go back to the same bad habits. Almost 2 years ago, I started a 1200 calorie food intake diet. I lost 35 pounds and felt really good of my accomplishment because I did it on my own. 5 months ago, I began to go back to an old habit of eating over 2200 calories a day!

When I began to notice the weight gain, I had to ask myself what allowed me to go back into an old habit? It was something that I had not yet conquered. Once I realized that thing that triggered an old habit. I immediately handled it in a way that I no longer made it an issue. I was able to get back on track but that experience also showed me that if I wanted to indulge in a slice of cheesecake every once in a while, it wouldn't mean that I was going back to bad things. While I understand this tool can be challenging as well, it's my belief that it will construct a distinction in your walk on your self-love journey!

11

ACCEPT PEOPLE IN your circle that have your greatest attentiveness at heart. Embracing people that love you unconditionally is a must. It is my opinion when dealing with people that has no interest in encouraging and uplifting you, their negative talk if you're not careful, will affect you in a way that it will discourage you and prevent you from moving forward in a POSITIVE way! I allowed a family member to bring me down with her actions and words for years, we grew up together so I really didn't want to believe this person just did not like me.

In my heart, I was hoping she was really for me and due to what she was going through it just made her that way. In reality, this person had a hate love type of relationship when it pertained to me. When I was in my dark space, I made the silly decision of entrusting this person with some hurtful things that transpired in my life.

Weeks later this person took to social media speaking of me in a way of dishonor! This was the true definition of toxicity! I made the conscious decision of ridding myself of this person! Did you know that loving people from a far is always an option? Believe me when I say, it will make your heart happy! Please understand the less negative people you have in your life the more you can focus on your journey to self love! I had to move forward in embarking on my self-love journey.

12

BREATHE. "AND THE Lord God formed man of the dust of the ground, and breathed into his nostrils the breath of life; and man became a living being..." (Genesis 2:7, KJV). It is my belief God would not have breathed into the nostrils of man if his intentions were not for us to have life.

We must be aware to know when it's time to sit, be still and just breathe with the understanding of knowing that God is in complete control of our situations and problems if we would just let go and let God! While doing this it gives opportunity for you to focus on where you're going in life and your plans of getting to where you need to be. When my anxiety level arises, my husband will look at me with his handsome admiring eyes and say "Babe just breathe".

When women are in labor and feel those contractions their significant other, coach or doctor will tell her "just breathe". According to Merriam-Webster dictionary Breathe simply means to draw air into and expel it from the lungs. To take oxygen and give out carbon dioxide through natural processes. Without breath we perish. On this self-love journey perishing is no longer an option. It doesn't matter what you're going through do not allow your circumstances to make you feel dead within. Rise up from your conditions and Breathe.

13

COMMEMORATE WITH HONORING yourself. I often joke about being my worst critic but in reality, it was the truth. How many of us often turn our attention to all the wrong things going on in and around us as oppose to indulging in all the good things? How many of us honor and celebrate others whether its attending birthday parties, job promotions, marriages and many more?

Honoring yourself is having compassion within as Jesus had compassion for us all. "But when he saw the multitudes, he was moved with compassion for them, because they were weary and scattered, like sheep having no Sheppard..." (Matthew 9:36, KJV). How much more should we honor ourselves? Start celebrating yourself with knowing it will be beneficial in helping you on this wonderful journey to self-love. One thing I have learned, if you wait for people to honor you in your own timing, you could possibly set yourself up for disappointment! I love my children with all my heart.

However, every year after turning 40, I tell my children how I would love to have a beautiful well decorated huge birthday party because I never had one and I feel that it would be a beautiful thing for my children to plan something just for ME. Needless to say, I never got that birthday party or dinner but I decided to plan my own Birthday dinner because I realized that its ok to honor and celebrate yourself! I'm not saying plan your own birthday party from now on, I'm simply saying STOP waiting for others to honor you.

HONOR yourself. Love, honor and respect yourself. find worthiness within because you are deserving of it. Nurture your own needs with the understanding that you're not being egocentric, you're choosing to put your needs foremost.

14

BE A BLESSING to other people. "He who has a generous eye will be blessed, for he gives of his bread to the poor..." (Proverbs 22:9, KJV). It is my opinion that God requires us to be a blessing to others. Please understand being a blessing does not always include monetary gifts!

Being a blessing consists of praying for others with sincerity in your heart for people. Being of encouragement to someone gives him or her the courage and confidence needed to get out of the situation or circumstances in which their facing. We are in a world of technology which makes it easier contacting people from all over. I summons you to commit yourself in being a blessing to someone at least once a week whether it's texting or using social media platforms. Look over someone for you never know the severity of ones affairs!

15

———

BE THANKFUL. "IN everything give thanks for this is the will of God in Christ Jesus for you..." (1 Thessalonians 5:18, KJV). I belief its of importance to God that we have a gratitude of thanks. Pursue the pattern of allowing oneself of being grateful in all things. Choosing to live a life of gratitude is momentous in living well! Throughout my day, I make sure to give thanks unto God in knowing that if it had not been for him, I would have never allowed myself to see a way out of the darkness I was in so very deeply. I have also learned to be grateful even in the small things because small things can turn into big things if you are humbled enough to receive it.

I have been through a lot of test, trials and storms yet I am grateful for it because it has made me the woman I am today. It has allowed me to value, love and enjoy my life the way which God intended for me!

I will forever be thankful of the fact my husband and myself, chose not to divorce! We would've lost the opportunity to see how much our marriage was worth sacrificing! We are far from perfect, but we have an understanding in knowing that no matter what we endure, we're in it till the very end because our love is everlasting!

I'm sharing this with my readers because I believe that we all go through something in life but the way in which you choose to handle it, determine the outcome!

16

SELF-EXAMINATION. ACCORDING TO Merriam-Webster dictionary self-examination is a reflective examination (as one's beliefs and motives). Have you ever questioned yourself about the things you do and why you do them?

Do you really take time in reflecting on the moves you made in life and ways in which they were beneficial to you? Enhancing our ability to understand ourselves and our motivations and to learn more about our own values helps us take the power away from the distractions of our modern, face-paced lives and instead refocus on fulfillment (Wood, 2013). "Examine yourself as to whether you are in faith. Test yourself. Do you not know yourself, that Jesus Christ is in you? Unless indeed you are disqualified..." (2 Corinthians 13:5, KJV).

I believe God wants us to examine ourselves for a reason for we should never think highly of ourselves in a way that brings destruction to our well-being. I believe the reason why we may lack in this area because we are afraid of what we may find out about US. However, in order for us to continue this journey, self-examination is imperative because it's an opportunity for change. Periodically my husband will tell me how proud he is and how much I have grown. This is because I made the decision to examine everything about myself good and bad. I had to get down to the very core of my being and that was rather difficult to do yet, it helped me grow and mature. In self-examination you will detect in which your powerful in loving yourself and at which place your fragile!

17

TAKE CONTROL OVER your thought life. Did you know that you are in complete control over your thoughts? We must realize and understand that negative thoughts will arise. However, we have the authority to cancel all negative thoughts from our mind. How often do we dwell on negative thoughts? Allow oneself to practice on minimizing the negative and focus more on the positive because the negative thoughts can put you in a state of mind that can affect your whole being.

We are now in a new year which could mean a new way of living. How are you choosing to live your life? I feel that I have come a long way within my life and the way in which I now choose to live it for the remaining of the time God will allow me to be here.

In other words, I refuse to waste time on anything or anyone that's not bringing positive vibes because I have come to far to go backwards. God gave me something very special and my mission is to share my testimonies in hopes of being a part of changing lives in a positive way. God loves us all, lets embrace Gods love by loving one another and being of encouragement because we never know who needs a touch of the capabilities of living free and staying FREE.

18

PRACTICE ON BEING consistent. Adore yourself enough with the belief in completing whatever it is you set your mind into doing. When I started doing seminars, I was very consistent in making sure I did my research pertaining to the topic as well as being prompt in hosting. However, once I began to work on my online business, the consistency of my seminars diminished and the drive to do it was gone. I never had time to study or research because I allowed all my time and energy be put in this business in which I just started so it required lots of time.

It is my perception that being consistent will also allow you to see your capabilities in given 100 percent in doing something you enjoy for self.

I have since resumed my live free be free seminars as I am aware of the need in not only being consistent yet, remaining consistent!

19

EXERCISE. IT'S OF great import that we exercise even if walking around the neighborhood for 30 minutes a day. This allows your mood to improve because you will feel happy that you're doing something so relaxing and enjoyable.

There are many benefits in exercising losing weight and possible prevention in high blood pressure or diabetes to name a few. Some people may feel that exercising is boring, therefore I would suggest going with a friend or group of people to make it more of a commitment for yourself.

20
———

DELETE THE WORD depression from your vocabulary. I know firsthand the importance of deleting depression from your mind and being. To be in a depressive state gives permission for your thoughts to be negative and may ultimately become unhealthy in your self love journey. Theres no good thing in being depressed. Yet, there are ways in dealing with this vicious word that helps keep you stabilized.

Some may need to seek a therapist or perhaps medication to even out the balance within your mind of having such negative thoughts about your life, some may even turn to drugs for comfort. Being depressed could lead to suicidal thoughts or attempts! You may feel there's no way out. You may feel alone, sad or even lonely! But, I am a living testimony that overcoming depression can be achieved! Depression is not of God and we must choose to deposit positive words within our spirits. We must choose to live and not perish. We must choose to live free be free and remain free.

Printed in the United States
by Baker & Taylor Publisher Services